ELSTON ©

ELSTON

BACK TO THE DRAWING BOARD

POLESTAR
BOOK PUBLISHERS

Published by
Polestar Press Ltd., P.O. Box 69382, Station K, Vancouver, BC V5K 4W6

Distributed by
Raincoast Books, 112 East Third Avenue, Vancouver, BC, V5T 1C8 (604) 873-6581

Canadian Cataloguing in Publication Data
Elston, Dave, 1958–
Back to the drawing board
ISBN 0-919591-71-X

1. Sports—Caricatures and cartoons. 2. Canadian
wit and humor, Pictorial. I. Title.
NC1449.E48A4 1991   741.5'971   C91-091588-1

Acknowledgements
Special thanks to Bill Davidson for helping out with the by-lines.

These cartoons previously appeared in the *Calgary Sun, Edmonton Sun,
The Hockey News,* or *Inside Hockey.*

Printed in Canada

CONTENTS

PICTURE FROM THE THEOREN FLEURY HELMET-CAM

This collection of cartoons is dedicated to the memory of Aunt Sal.

HOCKEY
THE 1990–91 REGULAR SEASON

SEPTEMBER 27, 1990:   GOALIE GRANT FUHR RECEIVES A ONE-YEAR
SUSPENSION FOR COCAINE USE.

SEPTEMBER 1990:

AL MACINNIS SIGNS A $4 MILLION, 4-YEAR
CONTRACT WITH THE CALGARY FLAMES.

THE OILERS' VERSION OF GETTING YOUR HAIR "MOOSED".

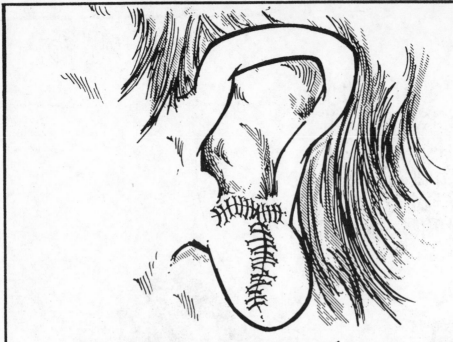

23

BROWN-NOSING

JANUARY 19, 1991: NHL ALL-STAR GAME IN CHICAGO STADIUM,
CAMPBELL CONFERENCE 11, WALES CONFERENCE 5.

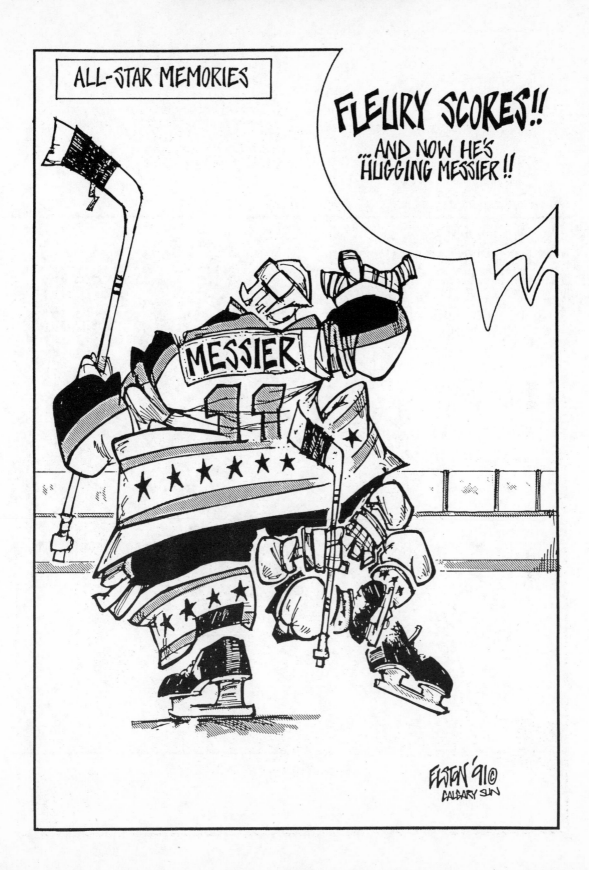

OWNER PETER POCKLINGTON GIVES EVERYONE ON THE STANLEY CUP CHAMPION EDMONTON OILERS DIAMOND RINGS. ALAS, THEN-ASSISTANT COACHES JOHN MUCKLER, TED GREEN AND ALL THE TRAINING STAFF DISCOVER THEIR DIAMONDS ARE FAKE.

FEBRUARY 18, 1991: GRANT FUHR RETURNS TO THE NHL.

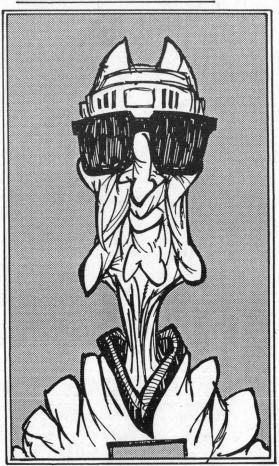

DAVE TAYLOR

LARRY ROBINSON

BRUCE McNALL'S VERSION OF "THE CALIFORNIA RAISINS."

42

BASEBALL

ELSTON AT BAT

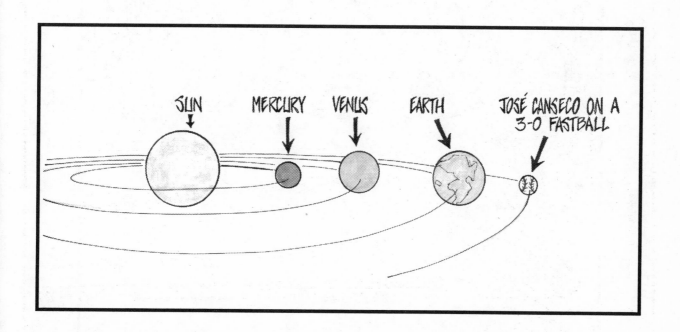

APRIL, 1985: A SPRING SNOWSTORM WELCOMES TRIPLE-A BASEBALL TO CALGARY.

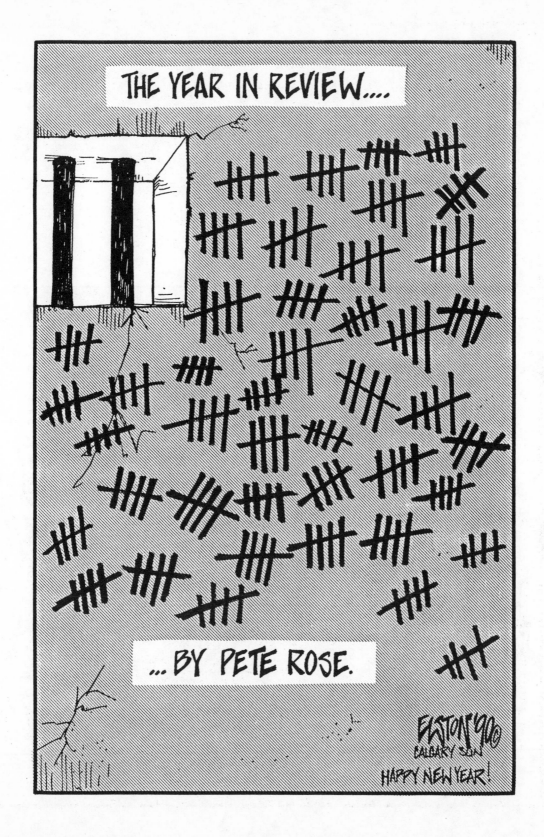

THE LAST TIME THE CUBS WON
THE WORLD SERIES

BOSTON, 1989

RECENT PORTRAIT OF THE MONTREAL EXPOS' PITCHING STAFF

THE END OF THE 1990 MAJOR LEAGUE BASEBALL LOCKOUT

PLAYOFFS, 1989

THE OAKLAND BAT-BOY
PICKING UP AFTER
JOSÉ CANSECO

LENNY DYKSTRA DRIVING IN A RUN

OCTOBER 17, 1989: OAKLAND, CALIFORNIA — WORLD SERIES
INTERRUPTED BY EARTHQUAKE.

WIDE WORLD OF ELSTON

THE MILK AND COOKIES
AT GEORGE FOREMAN'S PLACE

ELSTON '90©
CALGARY SUN

THE GEEZERS AT CAESARS

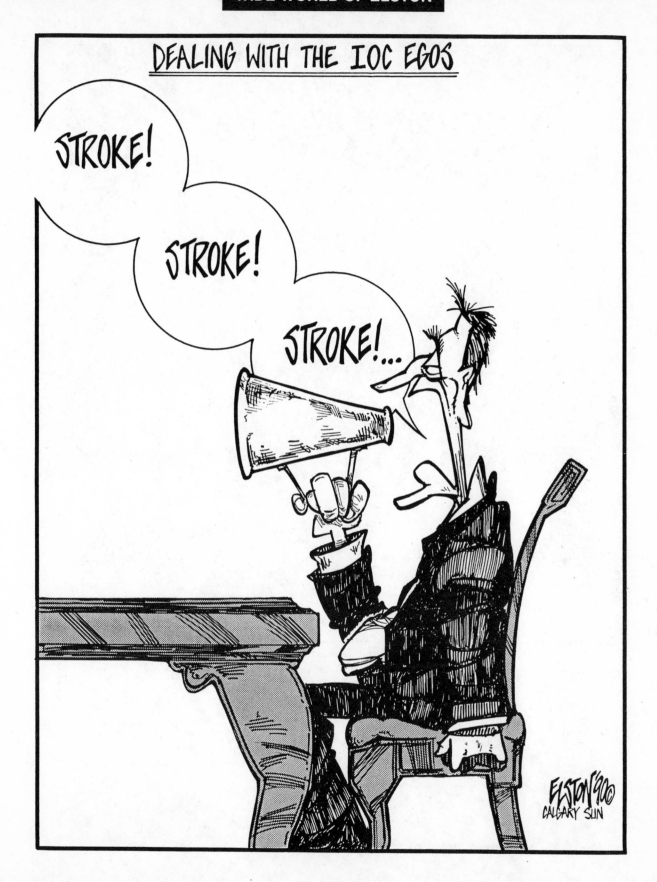

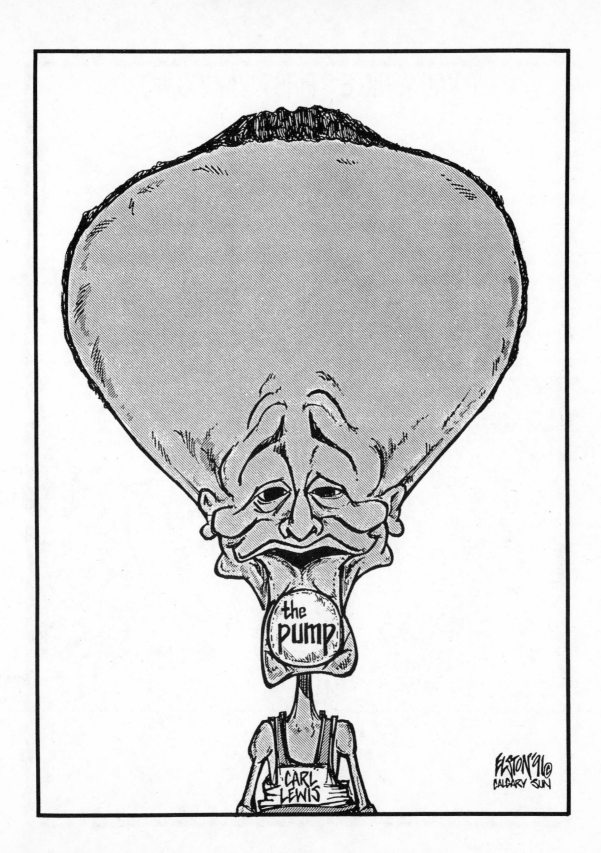

JANUARY 17, 1991: THE GULF WAR BEGINS

HE KNOWS IF YOU'VE BEEN SLEEPING,
HE KNOWS WHEN YOU'RE AWAKE,
HE KNOWS IF YOU'VE BEEN BAD OR GOOD....

ELSTON '89 ©
CALGARY SUN

....BO KNOWS CHRISTMAS!

STEROIDS
PERFORMANCE-ENHANCING CARTOONS

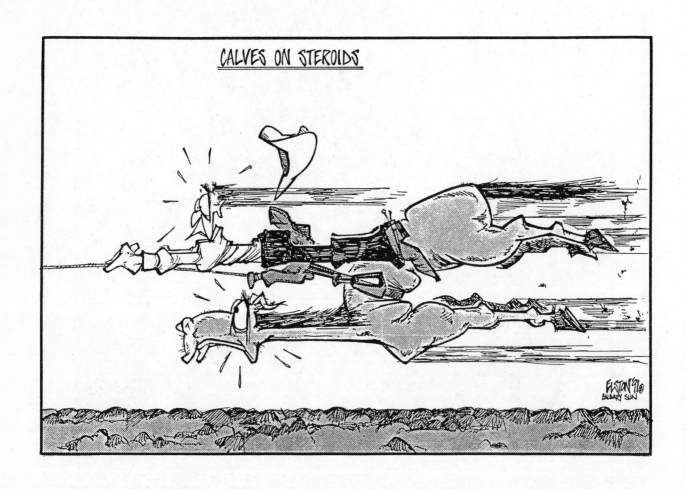

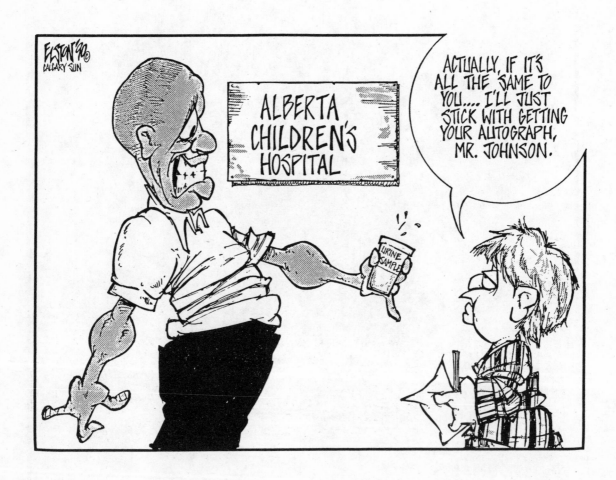

FOOTBALL
CFL FOLLIES

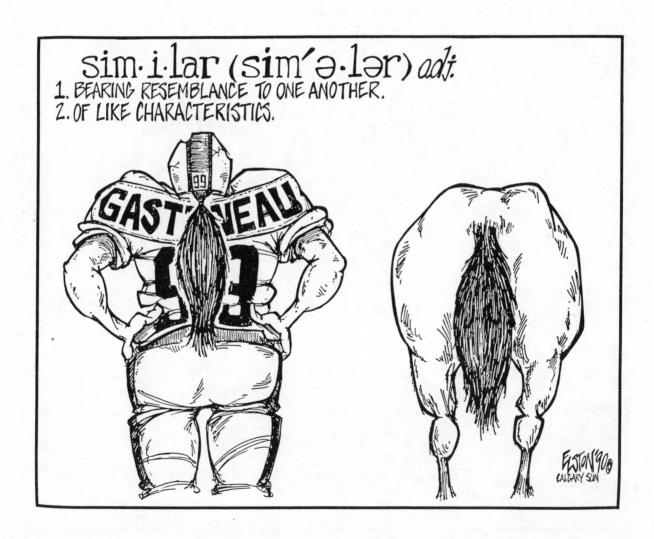

THE SKYDOME EXPERIENCES PROBLEMS MAKING THE CONVERSION FROM BASEBALL TO FOOTBALL.

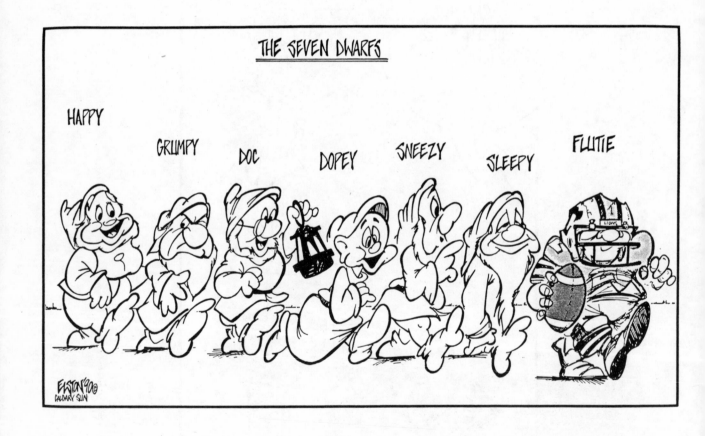

THE SACRIFICIAL LAMB

NOVEMBER 20, 1989:
CFL WESTERN FINAL

SASKATCHEWAN - 32
EDMONTON - 21

DRAWING THE SASKATCHEWAN ROUGHRIDERS OFFSIDE

SEPTEMBER 3, 1990:
LABOR DAY CLASSIC IN CALGARY:

EDMONTON - 38
STAMPEDERS - 4

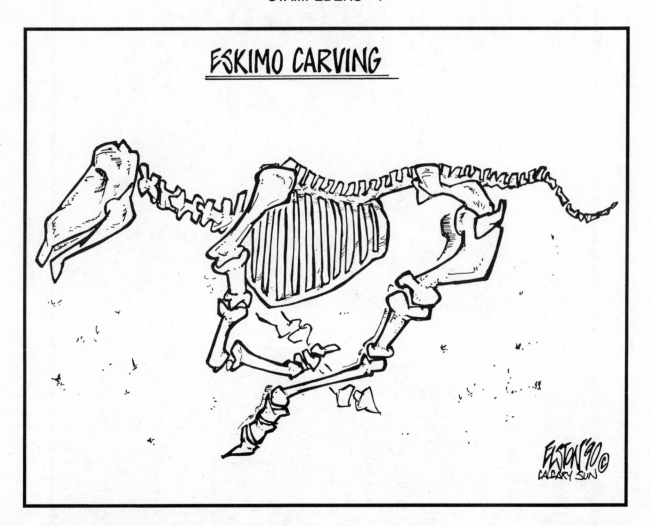

ESKIMO CARVING

THE RIDERS DIP INTO THE FREE AGENT MARKET

HOCKEY

HIGHLIGHTS FROM THE 1991 PLAYOFFS

FLAMES BOW OUT AFTER THE FIRST ROUND.

MAY, 1991: PENGUINS BEAT THE BRUINS.